20
KEYS TO A *SUCCESSFUL*
MARRIAGE
IN THE 21ST CENTURY

20 Keys To A Successful Marriage In The 21st Century

Copyright © 2019 by Carlton and Rev. Theresa Dunston
Divine Destiny and Purpose Ministries, LLC

All rights reserved.
This book may not be reproduced, in whole or in part, without written permission from the publisher, except by a reviewer who may quote brief passages in a review; nor may any part of this book be reproduced, stored in a retrieval system, or transmitted in any form or by any means, electronic, mechanical, recording or other, without written permission from the publisher.

For information, interviews or booking contact
ddp.ministries@yahoo.com

FIRST EDITION

Unless otherwise stated, Scripture was taken from various versions of the HOLY BIBLE

ISBN: 978-1-7331760-0-2 (paperback)
ISBN: 978-1-7331760-1-9 (ebook)

20
KEYS TO A SUCCESSFUL
MARRIAGE
IN THE 21ST CENTURY

**CARLTON &
REV. THERESA DUNSTON**

Dedication

We dedicate this book to our parents, Carlton R. Dunston, Sr., and Marsha Hayes; and Charles E. Waters, Jr. (deceased), and Dr. Patricia D. Hatten (deceased). Our parents were our first example of marriage and modeled before us the challenge of the covenant. We thank our parents for supporting us as we committed to marriage as young adults, and for encouraging and praying for us along the way during those times when we wanted to quit and give up on our marriage. To our children, Hakeem C. Dunston, Cierra R. Dunston, and Kayla Mae Dunston (daughter-in-law), this is our legacy to you. We pray that this book will bless you, enlighten you, and assist you with navigating through your own marital journey. To our unborn grandchildren, we dedicate this book as a token of our love and legacy to you.

TABLE OF CONTENTS

Foreword by Rev. Dr. Cassandra Young Marcus ix

Acknowledgments xiii

Introduction xv

Key #1: Divorce Is Not Our Option 1

Key #2: Marriage Is Not 50/50 7

Key #3: Your Spouse Does Not Complete You 11

Key #4: Practice Forgiveness Daily 17

Key #5: Don't Allow Resentment To Take Root 23

Key #6: Be Intentional About Understanding
Each Other's Love Language 27

Key #7: Share Your Dreams, Goals, And
Aspirations With Your Spouse 33

Key #8: Talk About The Future With Your Spouse 37

Key #9: Keep The Lines Of Communication
Open With Your Spouse 41

Key #10: Take The Time To Learn And Know
Each Other's Needs In The Marriage 47

Key #11: Listen Instead Of Thinking.................................53

Key #12: Don't Keep Secrets: Practice Transparency.........57

Key #13: Stay Romantic 63

Key #14: Date Your Spouse Regularly 69

Key #15: Maintain The Mindset That
Spending Time Together Is Important 73

Key #16: Express Love And Affection
Towards Your Spouse Daily...77

Key #17: Compliment Each Other Often 81

Key #18: Never Go To Bed Angry 87

Key #19: Have A Vision Statement For
Your Marriage..91

Key #20: Prioritize Prayer In Your Marriage
(His View) 99

Key #20: Prioritize Prayer In Your Marriage
(Her View)... 105

Foreword

Through the years I have observed the conscientious work of Carlton Dunston and the Rev. Theresa Waters-Dunston. This husband-and-wife team has passionately dedicated their lives to serving God and serving the people of God. For example, while serving as an associate minister at Turner Chapel African Methodist Episcopal Church in Marietta, GA, Theresa effectively facilitated premarital education sessions. She has extended this work as founder of Divine Destiny and Purpose Ministries, LLC. Both she and Carlton, through the use of social media, speak words of encouragement and empowerment to those who visit their forum. Out of their experience, having been married for 27 years and together for 31years, they have addressed marital concerns through social media and now in their book, 20 <u>Keys to a Successful Marriage in the 21st Century</u>. Their work is relevant to today's problem of divorce. According to the <u>Encyclopedia of Psychology,</u> 40 to 50 percent of married couples in the United States divorce. Whereas healthy marriages promote healthy couples and healthy children, Carlton and Theresa's 20 Keys demonstrate a worthy effort to promote healthy relationships and show how to avoid the unfortunate consequence of divorce.

Their format is simple. Having reflected upon their own experience and the work that they have done to maintain their vows, Carlton and Theresa present 20 Keys with the intention that their insight will help couples hold on to their vows and not give up. Their foundation is both experiential and biblical. They share scriptures, discourse, and prayers as they depict each key. More specifically, one problem addressed head-on is divorce. They state in the first chapter, "Divorce is Not Our Option." Soon the reader learns that this is their choice, with one exception to this rule. They are transparent about the challenges and mistakes that they have confronted on their marital journey. They do not pretend to have a perfect marriage. The reader soon discovers that Carlton and Theresa have relied heavily upon their faith in God to empower them to sustain their covenant.

The other keys portrayed in the book include, "Marriage is not 50/50," "Your Spouse does not Complete You," "Don't Keep Secrets: Practice Transparency," "Prioritize Prayer in Your Marriage," "Have a Vision Statement for your Marriage," as well as a depiction of 13 more keys.

Carlton and Theresa shared their vision statement for marriage and challenge couples to do the same. Their vision statement reads:

Dunston Marriage Vision Statement

We will have a God-centered marriage that is sustained by Respect, Love, Integrity, and Joy. Our marriage will exemplify Unity and Oneness, setting a Godly example for others to follow. We are committed to Encouraging, Supporting, and Praying for and with one another daily. We are dedicated to Nurturing and Strengthening our marriage by spending quality time with one another where true intimacy dwells. With the help of the Holy Spirit, we will honor the covenant we have made before God.

Carlton and Theresa speak generously from the heart, from their hearts to the reader's heart. The reader may come away with renewed vigor to make their marriage work. Carlton and Theresa frankly state that prayer and a willingness to work on the marriage, utilizing the keys that have worked for them, may strengthen and empower couples to experience a meaningful and healthy marriage.

The Rev. Dr. Cassandra Young Marcus, Co-Pastor
Turner Chapel A.M.E. Church
Marietta, GA

Acknowledgments

We give glory, honor, and praise to God who is and has been, the "I Am that I Am" in our lives and in our marriage. For God we live, and for God we die! We thank God for gifting us with purpose and destiny and for not giving up on us when we were out of alignment with the plan and purpose for our lives and our marriage covenant.

We are indebted to all those who acted as midwives and encouraged, prayed, instructed, and mentored us along the way as we made our way to the birthing position to push this baby out.

We thank our Mother in ministry, Rev. Dr. Cassandra Young Marcus, for writing a powerful foreword. You are and have been a true blessing and inspiration to us and our lives over the years.

To Rev. Dr. Kenneth E. Marcus who has gone home to be with our Lord, we praise God for you and every sermon you preached, every lesson you taught, and every prophetic word you spoke that compelled us to write this book.

To our graphic artist, Alfonso Ramirez, Artistic Revelations Designs, for creating our beautiful book cover; and Kenna O'Flannigan, All Things Scribal, for your editorial works on this manuscript-- your brilliant perspective and guidance remain priceless. You are both the crème de la crème.

To every pastor, prophet, prophetess, preacher, evangelist who spoke a word from God over our lives regarding our purpose and destiny, thank you for your obedience to God!

To every force that came against our marriage and every trial that tried to take us out, the pain of our past helped to inspire and push us to write this book.

Introduction

In 2016 we celebrated 25 years of marriage, otherwise referred to as **The Silver Anniversary**. To God be all the glory! Our 25th wedding anniversary was very significant for us, particularly since many of our peers doubted that our marriage would last since we married so young, and the fact that we are both the product of divorce. Today we are not afraid or too embarrassed to admit that we entered our marriage without a true model of what a healthy and prosperous marriage looked like or what a godly marriage looked like. We lacked a full understanding of the level of commitment and dedication required by the marriage covenant. Yes, we did engage in premarital counseling; however, we learned early on in our marriage that these sessions were not enough. These sessions were not designed to break through our embedded ideologies and predispositions of marriage.

Our marriage became our classroom. Early on in our marriage, we learned how to be married and how to stay married through our mistakes, through trial and error, and through the encouragement and advice we received from our loved ones. It was not until approximately 10 years into our marriage that we began to seek God wholeheartedly to understand and to experience a godly marriage. It was then that God accepted our invitation and began to renovate, restructure, and rebuild our marriage during some of the most tumultuous times as a married couple.

In 2016, in celebration of 25 years of marriage, we decided to identify 25 key principles that helped to transform our marriage into what it is today. We shared these principles, "25 Keys to a Successful Marriage in the 21st Century" via Facebook Live, and the response was overwhelming. It was after this that we realized there was a need for what we had to offer, and we had a book in the making. This book contains 20 of our most important keys.

We desire that this book will be a resource for married couples specifically, but couples in general. This book is designed to be used as a discussion tool to explore key biblical principles that are pertinent to the marriage covenant and can be used to evaluate, to rekindle, to strengthen, and to renew the marriage covenant.

"So they are no longer two, but one flesh. Therefore, what God has joined together, let no one separate."

(Matthew 19:6 **NIV**)

KEY #1

DIVORCE IS NOT OUR OPTION

Knowing your history can help you shape your destiny. At the tender age of ten when we first met, unbeknownst to us, both of our parents had separated and ultimately divorced around the same time. We were both dealing with these issues and had no idea that our lives were parallel and our pain mirrored that of the other. We see this as God's divine plan and divine appointment. God saw fit to introduce us at such a young age with a plan to later join us together as one. No one could design such a plan like our God. Until recently, we had not even acknowledged the awesomeness of God in our union. Through our spiritual journey together over the years, the more we matured, the more God began to provide us with greater revelation about our union. We were destined to be together, but little did we know we would have to fight to remain together.

In Matthew 19:6, we are reminded of God's perfect plan for the marriage covenant. The plan for two, husband and wife, to become united as one flesh, and God's desire that no marriage ends in divorce. Spouses have to make a conscious decision to honor God's original plan and not entertain or flirt with the idea of divorce. In this 21st century where the negative influences circulating through mass and social media are endless, couples have to work much harder at remaining committed to the marriage vows. It is one thing to write or recite *"What God joined together let not man separate,"* but the battle is won when couples have the fortitude to fight for their marriage during those difficult seasons when others would decide to quit.

On several occasions, I have been tempted and tested regarding our marriage vows. Mistakes have been made on both sides. We have faced issues from betrayal to financial woes and other struggles. We have said and done things that both of us have regretted. We have done things we said we would never do. We have had to confront the unhealthy and destructive marriage examples that were given to us. We have had to renew our faith and renew our vows. We have gone through marital counseling. But one thing we have never done is quit!

"Till Death Do Us Part." These five words are the final words spoken by couples as part of the traditional marriage vows. Couples recite these words in front of God, their family, and every other attendee that is a witness to their union during their wedding ceremony. Today I am not ashamed to say that when I recited these vows, I had no realistic idea of marriage or the trials and turbulence that would infiltrate our marriage and would come to challenge these vows. I entered

my marriage through the fairy tale lens of living happily ever after like the Huxtables, with expectations and anticipation of things I had only read about and seen portrayed on The Cosby Show. Therefore, I can honestly say that only God and the commitment to our vows is what helped to sustain us in my ignorance in the early years of marriage.

As previously stated, like many other married couples, my husband and I are both a product of divorce. Neither of us experienced or were exposed to a healthy, whole, and fulfilling marriage during our impressionable young years. We watched our parents' marriages crumble under the pressures and challenges of life, lacking role models and mentors that would and could have encouraged them to hold on and trust God in the midst of it all. So with this as our foundation, you can imagine that our journey to become one has been a roller coaster. Though the ride has been bumpy and scary, with God's help, we are determined to break the generational cycle of divorce and are continually building on a godly foundation that our children and grandchildren can stand on and even build upon for years to come.

"Divorce is Not Our Option" is the motto that we live by. We choose this every day. We are fully aware of the daily struggle and choice not only for us but for all couples to remain married, especially in this 21st century of reality TV. It is not easy to walk out the marriage vows amid turbulence and disappointment. But with God, godly mentors, and, if applicable, marriage counseling, it is more than possible.

Walking in love and forgiveness helps to heal wounded vows. It is possible to have a thriving marriage after failed expectations, sickness, loss, financial failures, betrayal, and even adultery. It takes the desire and commitment of both spouses to make it happen. I encourage husbands and wives to do whatever it takes to renew, repair, restore, and revive your marriage.

NOTE: If you are in a marriage that threatens your safety or wellbeing or that of your children or family, we encourage you to develop a Safety Plan. God is concerned about our welfare and does not expect us to subject ourselves to any form of abuse (financially/economically, physically, mentally, emotionally, verbally, or socially). God's perfect plan for marriage does not require us to remain in harm's way.

PRAYER

Lord, I lift up every marriage, asking that you would touch the husband and wife, anointing them from top to bottom. God, renew their minds and their hearts that the love that they have for one another would be enhanced and multiplied, in Jesus' name. Lord, you said that love covers. I pray that their love would cover every mistake, every mishap, and every issue and challenge that they have and will have to face. I declare that their marriage cannot and will not fail and shall not end in divorce. Lord, teach them your perfect plan for the marriage covenant and give them the tools and weapons to be used to overcome every plot and plan of the enemy against their union. Let their marriage legacy be one of a strong and godly foundation. Lord, we dedicate our marriages to you and thank you in advance for saving and healing our wounded vows, in Jesus' name. Amen.

Wow Moment Reflection

> *"Then God said, 'Let us make mankind in our image, in our likeness, so that they may rule over the fish in the sea and the birds in the sky, over the livestock and all the wild animals, and over all the creatures that move along the ground. So God created mankind in his own image, in the image of God he created them; male and female he created them."*

(Genesis 1:26-27 **NIV**)

KEY #2

MARRIAGE IS NOT 50/50

In today's society, we hear "marriage should be 50/50," with the concept of both individuals doing what is considered "their equal share." We hear "50/50," and most people immediately think both persons (husband and wife) doing their part makes a 100% functioning marriage. However, let's relate our thinking to the word of God in Genesis 1:26-27. God is telling us that He made mankind in His image and likeness, both male and female. So if that is true, can you tell God He should be okay with you giving him 50% of who you are? And is it alright that God gives you 50% of who He is? We should see our spouses as we see God. If we look at them in that form, we should be quite embarrassed to say or agree that we are only going to give 50% of who we are.

The world tells us that in our marriage we should have a 50/50 mindset, but is it true that marriage will work if I put my half in the pot of our relationship with the hopes that my spouse gives their half? I encourage you not to play word games with this and try to say, "Well, 50 over 50 is one whole, so what is the difference?" The difference is that the mindset of the 50/50 is not the whole number 50. It is the 50% concept, which is **HALF**. Then when you bring that discussion about what is lacking in the marriage to the table, the part that is lacking just may be the very thing you thought you were presenting as whole. We have to understand that when we get married, it is for us to become and act with a oneness mindset and spirituality.

Becoming one is bringing and presenting your whole you, not a piece of you. I often hear, "It is hard to connect with her!" and "She drives me crazy with the things that are so aggravating!" Then there is that, "He is so immature!" and "He never sees eye-to-eye with me!" How about the famous "You and I will never…!" From time to time we go in and out of phases in our marriage that are called difficulties, and, yes, these things make us separate our emotions from who we really are. We have to assure that what is being presented as one in our marriage is the whole you on both sides. Imagine how healthy of a married body your marriage would be if your union would be 100/100. If you look at it in numbers, that is 200%, and in my math, 200% is a whole lot more than 100%.

Do not give your half to the marriage. Give your whole to it and watch God match it! To take it a step further, if one of you is not well (health) and all that one has to give of their 100% is 75%, it is still their 75% that will represent their whole. At the end of the day, it is you giving all of you to your spouse. And again, when God says He created us in His likeness and in His image, how can you *not* give someone that resembles God, your all? Just keeping it 100 (one-hunned)!

PRAYER

Oh, Mighty God, Creator of mankind, Heaven and Earth! We come before you, Lord, saying thank you for allowing us to recognize who we are and whose we are today. We thank you, oh, Lord, for your grace and your tender mercy. We ask, oh, God, for an opening of heart and mind in understanding what marriage should be. You brought us together for a purpose and on purpose, and we will continue to let your light shine on us and through us. Create in us a new heart for each other, oh, Lord, so that we can present ourselves as a whole person for each other. As the songwriter said, 99 and a half won't do! It is ALL of who we are that we should be in our marriage, as well as what we bring. We thank you for wholeness and for oneness, in Jesus' name. Amen!

Wow Moment Reflection

"Therefore what God has joined together, let not man separate."

(Mark 10:9 **NKJV**)

KEY #3

YOUR SPOUSE DOES NOT COMPLETE YOU

Dictionary.com defines complete as" having all parts or elements; lacking nothing; whole; entire; full." *Dictionary Online* defines complete as "to make something whole or perfect." When I think of the title of this chapter, I immediately begin to think of the famous scene in the movie "Jerry Maguire" (1996). **"You Complete Me"** are the infamous words that were spoken by Tom Cruise across a living room filled with women to actress Renée Zellweger at the end of the movie, over 20 years ago. These words exemplified and signified true love, a perfect love, and sent hearts fluttering and imagining such a love for themselves. These three words created a myth and a new standard and measuring tool for persons seeking the love of their life.

"You Complete Me" implies that we are incomplete beings in need of someone else to make us whole. Although these words sound lovely and are music to our itching ears, the reality is that no one can complete us but God. When God created us, He created us whole. We are already a whole being, despite our flaws. Our spouse is a whole being. When you and your spouse come together, you are two whole beings coming together as one. Entering marriage with the fallacy that your spouse or even marriage will complete you is not only problematic, but it is unhealthy and is a set-up for a pressured and potentially failed marriage. This perspective makes one appear needy, reliant, and dependent upon another human being instead of God to become whole, complete, and happy. Expecting your spouse to complete you puts undeserving pressure and a level of responsibility on your spouse so weighty that, over time, will eventually cause him or her to fall short, to feel inadequate, to feel burdened, and to crumble. Our spouses were not created to complete us nor to bear the weight of that responsibility. A more realistic perspective of our spouse would be for him/her to complement us.

God's purpose for marriage is not for spouses to complete the other. God's purpose for marriage is to become one flesh. Mark 10:7-8 (NIV) states, "'For this reason a man will leave his father and mother and be united to his wife, and the *two* **will become** *one* **flesh.' So they are no longer two,** but one flesh" (emphasis added). Throughout your marriage, the goal is for you and your spouse to continuously strive for oneness in all that you do. Genesis 2:24 (NKJV) states, "Therefore a man shall leave his father and mother and be joined to his wife, and they shall become one flesh." When we enter marriage knowing that only God can complete us and our spouse can complement us, we are less likely to place unrealistic expectations on our spouse to make us a whole person.

Being married for 27+ years has taught me the value in seeking to understand marriage from a biblical perspective. I, too, at some point in my youth embraced the false perspective and bought into the myth that my husband would complete me. I did not realize what came with this viewpoint. I failed to realize that my peace, my joy, my happiness, my unhappiness, etc. would be unjustifiably placed solely in the hands of my husband based on the fallacy that he somehow had magical powers to make me whole. In retrospect, I can admit that early on in our marriage many of the challenges and disagreements we had were based upon this faulty expectation. As I matured spiritually and in age, I understood that my husband did not have the ability to complete me; but instead, marriage is the opportunity for both of us to develop/improve, to enhance our beings, and to evolve into our best selves individually and collectively.

PRAYER

God, we ask that you would bless every wife with the knowledge and acceptance that they are whole and complete individuals in and of themselves. Allow wives to come into the knowledge that their husband was not meant to, nor can their husband complete them. Help us to realize and embrace the truth that you alone are the only one that can complete us. We take every thought captive that has and will try to cause us to settle in low self-esteem and think less of ourselves. Remind us that we were created in your likeness and in your image. God, give us a true understanding of your purpose for our life and our marriage, in Jesus' name! Amen.

Wow Moment Reflection

> *"For if you forgive others their trespasses* [their reckless and willful sins], *your heavenly Father will also forgive you. But if you do not forgive others* [nurturing your hurt and anger with the result that it interferes with your relationship with God], *then your Father will not forgive your trespasses."*
>
> (Matthew 6:14-15 **AMP**)

KEY #4

PRACTICE FORGIVENESS DAILY

God's word tells us that God requires that we forgive others for their trespasses. The scripture does not indicate that we are to forgive others only in certain situations or under certain circumstances and conditions. Neither does the scripture indicate that we are only to forgive a specific person or persons, or that forgiveness is conditional. There is no qualifier attached to this command. The text definitively states that we are to FORGIVE others, which includes our spouses. We are to forgive our spouses for their offenses even after the commission of the unthinkable, the unexpected, and the despicable.

According to the *English Oxford Living Dictionaries* online, Forgive means "to stop feeling angry or resentful towards (someone) for an offence, flaw, or mistake." Forgiveness is one of the most difficult and challenging things to do. Many married couples struggle with truly forgiving their spouse.

Oftentimes in our humanness, we compartmentalize and place forgiveness in a box. We choose to commit to only forgiving our spouse for certain things, and we decide that there are other things that we simply cannot and will not forgive our spouse for. Unfortunately, as Kingdom husbands and wives, we do not have the option nor the luxury to choose what acts to forgive. Our mandate from God is to forgive regardless of the act. Our faith is rooted in love and forgiveness as demonstrated through Christ on the cross and after the resurrection.

I can recall early on in our marriage Carlton was not completely honest with me about his interactions with another female after such actions were exposed. Eventually, he shared the truth with me, and not only was I angry with him, but I vowed never to forgive him. My ability to trust him was compromised. I held on to my anger and unforgiveness for a very long time to the point that I would remind him of what he had done. Although he was totally at fault, my response was not justified. Holding on to my anger and unforgiveness was disobedient to God, and it also created division between us. I also believe that during my period of unforgiveness I was responsible for blocking and delaying the blessings God had in store for me, our marriage, and our children.

For us to overcome this challenging time in our marriage and for our marriage to continue to grow and be strengthened, I had to choose to forgive. Believe me, this was not an easy thing to do, and I really did not want to do it. I started by asking God to forgive me for my disobedience and for choosing not to forgive my husband. I shared my heartfelt emotions with God, and I asked God to help me and to show me how to forgive my husband so that our marriage could be strengthened, blessed, and we could be a witness to other married couples. This was a lengthy process, but with God's help, I have been able to walk through the path to forgiveness.

In a covenant marriage, each spouse under the guidance of the Holy Spirit must commit to developing a heart of forgiveness. Forgiveness is not something that we say; it is something that we do. It is something that we practice daily. It is something that we do not in our own strength, but with the strength that only comes from the Holy Spirit. Forgiveness is tied to our heart which is the center of our emotions.

PRAYER

God, teach us to walk in forgiveness. Remove our selfish motives and desires of the flesh that cause us to walk in unforgiveness. Remind us that forgiveness is a matter of the heart not of the head. We welcome the instruction and power of the Holy Spirit to guide, teach and to empower us to really forgive our spouse as God has forgiven us. Help us to practice forgiveness daily. As we walk in forgiveness allow our marriage to be strengthened, transformed, and healed. In Jesus' name! Amen.

Wow Moment Reflection

"Look after each other so that none of you fails to receive the grace of God. Watch out that no poisonous root of bitterness grows up to trouble you, corrupting many."

(Hebrews: 12:15 **NLT**)

KEY #5

DON'T ALLOW RESENTMENT TO TAKE ROOT

Resentment is that thing that can eat through you from the inside out. It happens when someone deeply hurts, offends, or disappoints you, and you allow it to gnaw, penetrate and grow in your heart. This creates the entryway for resentment and bitterness to take root. Unresolved hurt, disappointment, or conflict is likely to result in resentment. Resentment is a buildup of other unresolved feelings and emotions in response to your spouse's behavior, actions, conduct, or inaction. Unforgiveness leads to resentment which, left unattended, ultimately begets hatred. All of these are sinful"...

How does resentment look and manifest itself? Resentment is that thing that causes you to rehearse, to recall, and to remind your spouse what they failed to do, what they did, when they did it, how you felt when they did it, and the consequences of it. Resentment is that emotion that causes you, at any given moment, to look at your spouse and get mad all over again about what he or she did in the past as if it just happened. Consequently, this unchecked emotion causes you to mistreat your spouse at any given time for any reason or for no reason at all.

There was a time in my marriage when I can now shamefully admit that I totally resented my husband. This resentment was rooted in my disappointment in him, in his professional accomplishments, and in what I believed was his lack of ambition. I felt as if he had failed to fulfill his end of our agreement and I had done just the opposite. You may be asking, *What agreement?* My response is, the agreements we made early on in our relationship and in our marriage. We had lengthy conversations about our life together, what we wanted it to look like, and how we would get there. We talked about our hopes and dreams for ourselves, our careers, our marriage, and our family. My issue was that when I looked at our life and our family, it did not resemble what we so artistically crafted in our minds. At this time in our marriage, I had concluded that my husband was living beneath his God-given gifts and abilities and had made a conscious decision not to give me (his wife) or our children his best. I felt as if he had settled for where he was, what we had, and that was that. I never took the time to have a healthy discussion with my husband about my thoughts or my feelings, or even his. Over time, my disappointment evolved into anger, and my anger became resentment. I didn't consider or even care at the time that my husband had been laid off for some years and potentially could have been having an internal struggle based on this dynamic. I carried this resentment for too long and lost precious time not being happy, joyful, grateful, and fully supportive of my husband. I was consumed in my feeling of resentment, and my actions showed it.

As women, we carry a place of power in our marriage that can be extremely beneficial or extremely detrimental. We get to choose daily which emotions we will reside in. I have learned that a resentful woman is not a nice woman and can destroy the very thing that God gave her.

PRAYER

God, we come seeking you for a mighty move of your Spirit. We ask you for forgiveness for harboring resentment and anger in our hearts towards our spouse. We stand in the gap for every marriage that is under attack and is battling with resentment, in Jesus' name. God, give every wife and give every husband the mind of Christ that will enable us to walk in love, forgiveness, and peace. We ask that you create in us a clean heart and renew a right spirit within. We renounce every spirit of resentment, hatred, and bitterness that has been running rampant in our marriage. We release the spirit of love, joy, and peace. We plead the blood of Jesus over our minds and our hearts that we would be cleansed and renewed so that our marriage would be repositioned and placed in right alignment with your will. We thank you for hearing and answering our prayer in Jesus' name. Amen!

Wow Moment Reflection

> *"Love is patient and kind; love does not envy or boast; it is not arrogant or rude. It does not insist on its own way; it is not irritable or resentful; it does not rejoice at wrongdoing, but rejoices with the truth. Love bears all things, believes all things, hopes all things, endures all things."*
>
> (1 Corinthians 13:4-7 **ESV**)

KEY #6

BE INTENTIONAL ABOUT UNDERSTANDING EACH OTHER'S LOVE LANGUAGE

As Christians, we always seem to find a way to incorporate 1 Corinthians 13 in our thinking related to love, but we refer to it when it comes to people like family members and even friends. Is God making it clear to us who this word should be referenced? No, He is not, because it is a word that relates to how we should be with our love, period. When it comes to our spouse, this scripture should be posted not just on Facebook, bathroom mirrors, or wherever you post scriptures, but this scripture should be evident all over your marriage.

First, "Love is patient." What is patient? <u>Patient</u> is defined as "able to accept or tolerate delays, problems, or suffering without becoming annoyed or anxious." Ultimately, God is saying that we need to be able to love each other, and in this case, love our spouse, with the ability to not be annoyed and to tolerate those things that come. Annoyed is another word for aggravated. When we really look at what causes us to be aggravated, we will truly find our problem is really us and not our spouse. We are aggravated because they remind us of the things we need to remember to do. We are aggravated because they find the faults that we have that are clearly obvious, even to us. So patience is something that we also need people to have with us.

Second, "Love is kind." Is God simply saying, treat each other with respect and care for each other? We should really be able to show kindness to our spouse simply because it is what our love should display. Yes, again, we have our moments of being annoyed and even angry, but love overrides anger every time. The rest of the scriptures speaks to what love is not, such as being rude. Oftentimes we can find ourselves engaging in the famous sarcastic remarks, or even doing or saying things without thinking of how our spouse will receive it. We must remember that we are two different people that are united together as one. Therefore, we have to pay attention to how our spouse views things as well as receives them. We cannot force our views on our spouse. They are who they are, which makes us whole or complete with them in our lives.

Let's talk about the 5 Love Languages (**Words of Affirmation, Quality Time, Receiving of Gifts, Acts of Service, and Physical Touch**). Words of Affirmation is that "I love you" and other compliments like, "You really look nice/beautiful today" statements. A person who requires this love language holds significant value to words. Quality Time is truly about giving the other person your undivided attention (refer to Key #15). This individual's love language is far from words of affirmation, because words to them are just words, especially when you cannot back them up. Quality time is giving them a level of satisfaction, comfort, and understanding that you are only focused on them. Receiving Gifts is built around the idea of tangible gifts. Some individuals find that receiving gifts from someone as the primary way they feel appreciated and loved. They see it as if, you love me enough to spend money on me or even for me, which is an awesome thing. Let's be clear though. The gifts have to be both meaningful and thoughtful. It does not make them a materialistic person or, as we call them, "gold diggers." It is merely their view on what lets them know or feel you love them.

Acts of Service is another form of actions speaking louder than words. They are looking for someone to help them in trying times. Therefore, be prepared to follow through with what you say you will do for them (no broken promises). Then Physical Touch is where you do exactly what its name is, "physical touching." Let's make it clear right at the beginning. "Physical Touch" is not defined as sexual or bedroom activities. This individual enjoys holding hands, kisses, hugs, and anything related to physical contact.

So I agree entirely that these are truly good to focus on when it comes to the direct understanding of what your spouse desires. Make sure this is a conversation that you have early on to get clear on what is needed, instead of doing things the way you think they should be done to show your spouse love. In closing, remember that applying godly, biblical instructions work through all of these languages. You cannot display any of the languages without patience and kindness. You clearly cannot do any of them if you are rude or arrogant. Love is God, and God has given us His ingredients as to how we are to love each other in our marriages.

PRAYER

Gracious and all-loving God, we thank you for your love and your joy. We ask, oh, God, that as you have displayed love to us for the sacrifice on the cross, that we first show you our love and gratitude. Oh, God, give us the ability to love our spouse the way Christ loved the church. That is the real love language that we should follow. But, oh, God, allow us to understand what it is that each of us needs within the act of love and the feeling of love. Your word tells us to be patient, be kind, and not to be arrogant or rude. So align our hearts with your word and keep us from the tricks and schemes of the enemy as we love our spouse. Cover the love. Cover the joy. Cover the marriage in the name of Jesus. Amen!

Wow Moment Reflection

> *"And the Lord God said, It is not good that the man should be alone; I will make him an help meet for him."*

(Genesis 2:18 **KJV**)

KEY #7

SHARE YOUR DREAMS, GOALS, AND ASPIRATIONS WITH YOUR SPOUSE

Genesis 2:18 reminds us that we serve a God of purpose. God is the giver of purpose. As Kingdom men and women, we must never forget that our God operates and creates out of purpose. Even the biblical text is permeated with the overall theme that everything God did and everything God created was for a specific purpose. Therefore, it rings true that the purpose of a person or thing preceded the person or thing itself. God does not identify purpose after God creates; instead, God creates a thing or person to fulfill a specific purpose. In light of this, we must embrace the fact that the covenant of marriage and the husband and wife were both created for a purpose.

In Genesis 2:18 the Hebrew word translated "help" is *'ezer,* and it means "to aid or help." According to *Strong's Concordance of the Bible*, the Hebrew word translated "meet" is *neged* and means "a front, i.e.,, part opposite; spec. a counterpart, or mate." The *Oxford Dictionary* defines helpmate as "A helpful companion or partner, especially one's husband or wife."

Whether we are considering the biblical interpretation or the dictionary definition, we find that a helpmate/help meet is one purposed to help or aid another. This does not equate to being his mother. I am sure you have heard the saying, "behind every successful man lies a woman." This is certainly true for the believer.

As wives walking in our God-ordained purpose as a helpmate/help meet to our husbands, we have a powerful and influential role in his overall success in life. As women, God has gifted us with the ability to not only hear and see the vision but to be what our husbands need us to be for the vision to manifest in our husband's life. Being a helpmate includes providing our husbands with whatever he needs (i.e., prayer, encouragement, support, resources, suggestions, listening, communicating, etc.) to carry out his God-given purpose. God has entrusted women with this assignment because God knows that we were given the innate ability to fulfill this assignment. As wives, we should not do this begrudgingly or out of obligation, but we should do it with confidence, willingness, and love, embracing the God-given power that lives within.

Although scripture states that the woman was created to be a helpmate, it does not mean that being a helpmate is one-sided. This is very much reciprocal. The husband in turn also has the responsibility to be what his wife requires of him in order to aid, help, or assist her in carrying out her own God-given purpose. In essence, ideally in covenant marriages, husbands and wives can and will accomplish what they were purposed for TOGETHER and will be a threat to the enemy!!!

PRAYER

Lord, we come thanking you for our spouse and the purpose that lies within them. We thank you for the purpose we share individually and collectively. We thank you that we are better together as a married couple than we are separate. We thank you that our purpose is intertwined in you and intertwined in who you purposed us to be as a Kingdom couple. Lord, help us to entrust our spouse with our goals, aspirations, and wildest dreams. Teach us how to be a helpmate to one another. Teach us how to be what our spouse needs us to be as they pursue their God-given purpose, dreams, and goals. Teach us how to pray for and over our spouse daily in a world that's evil and unfair and where dream and purpose killers reside. Lord, help us to remain faithful and to trust in you when it seems like the fulfillment of our purpose is taking much longer than we expected. Remind us that you operate outside of time, and a day with you is like a thousand years. Remind us that all of your promises are yea and amen! In Jesus' name we pray. Amen.

Wow Moment Reflection

*"For I know the plans I have for you, declares the Lord, plans to prosper you and not to harm you, plans to give you hope and a **_future_**."*

(Jeremiah 29:11 **NIV** *emphasis added*)

KEY #8

TALK ABOUT THE FUTURE WITH YOUR SPOUSE

Most of us have been asked in job interviews, "Where do you see yourself in the next five years?" The way we put together our own five-year plan for our life, we should have the same intentionality within our marriage. We not only have to put together a future plan with one another, but we should talk to each other about that plan or that vision constantly. When you purposefully sit down with each other and talk about the future, it provides a secure system for your spouse to feel that you see the marriage lasting. One of the things that God tells us in Jeremiah 29:11 is that He has a plan for us as His children to have a "future." In that, we have a firm belief that God has a vision of us having a lasting life from our present time. Giving each other the feeling that says, "I plan to be with you in the future" plays a great deal in the marriage.

We see it all the time how quickly marriages are ending. Part of it is because there is no vision of what the future will look like with one another. Businesses put together vision statements to know where they are going and the purpose of why they exist, so why not create a vision statement for your marriage. Theresa and I have conducted premarital education with couples who desire to get married. One of the tasks that are given to each couple is to create a "Vision Statement." They are to sit down together and decide what they want their lives to look like together and what they will commit to stand on. God's word (scripture) is always part of the vision and should be implemented into the vision statement. But the vision statement should also reflect what each spouse desires in the marriage's future. (See Key #19 for details about writing a vision statement).

Of course, over time the plan will change, and life will alter the vision statement. But we should never take away the future concept of our marriage. We see all the time with technology updates, does Microsoft or Apple shut its business down? No, they figure out a way to make things work for the time that technology is elevating too. We should do the same. As we update ourselves or, in other words, grow, we should figure out a way to make the marriage work for the new elevation we are headed to. Talk about vacation locations. Talk about the grandchildren and great-grandchildren. Talk about retirement and spending quality time. And talk about simply growing old together. What will that look like for you? Whenever Theresa and I talk about our future plans or desires together, it always gives me a sense that she sees us in the future **TOGETHER**. The word of God in Habakkuk 2:2 says, "And the LORD answered me, and said, Write the vision, and make it plain upon tables, that he may run that readeth it." However, in this case, do not just write it; TALK ABOUT IT, too!

PRAYER

Oh, Mighty and Gracious God, we come before you first seeking and asking for your forgiveness and humbling ourselves that those sins would be cast into the sea of forgetfulness. We thank you, oh, merciful God, for your word in Jeremiah 29:11 that tells us all about YOUR plans. We know that you are not like man that you would lie, so we know your plan is always prevailing in ourselves. Even when we cannot see it happening, we know the manifestation of it will come to pass. As we surrender to your will and your way, we ask, oh, Lord, that because your word tells us that your plans are to give us a hope and a future, that we continue to speak our future into existence for our marriage, our union, and our family. Thank you, God, for giving us the authority to say so! In Jesus' name, Amen!

Wow Moment Reflection

"Do not let unwholesome [foul, profane, worthless, vulgar] words ever come out of your mouth, but only such speech as is good for building up others, according to the need *and* the occasion, so that it will be a blessing to those who hear [you speak]."

(Ephesians 4:29 **AMP**)

KEY #9

KEEP THE LINES OF COMMUNICATION OPEN WITH YOUR SPOUSE

Communication in the marriage covenant is part of God's plan. Good communication can be a significant factor in making your marriage GREAT! Proverbs 29:5 states that a word spoken at the right (correct) time is like gold apples in the setting of silver. With a mindset of keeping the lines of communication open, we learn to think before we speak. In our marriages, we want to practice speaking the right thing at the right or correct time to minimize miscommunication. We want to avoid mishaps of speaking out of turn or even out of our feelings and emotions, both of which can be detrimental to our marriage. It is very difficult to take back our words once we have released them out of our mouths. As the bible clearly states, the tongue is powerful, and our words speak death or life. As women, we must admit that we can use our tongue to build our husbands up or tear them down. Our job is to stroke their ego and help them evolve into the Kingdom Man God designed them to be!

Oxforddictionaries.com defines communication as "the imparting or exchanging of information by speaking, writing, or using some other medium." In communication, HOW matters. It's not what we say, but how we (verbally/non-verbally) say it. Communication includes various components. According to H. Norman Wright and Wes Roberts in *Before You Say "I Do,"* communication consists of verbal (words) 7%, non-verbal (body language, eye contact, and facial expression) 55%, and tone (38%). Because of these three components, confusing/conflicting messages can be sent during the communication process. Experts agree that non-verbal is the most prominent part of our communication system. Therefore, we must be most conscious and aware of our non-verbal communication as we strive to strengthen this area in our marriage.

We believe that communication is one of the most critical factors in a marriage and can either contribute to building up or tearing down the marriage covenant. In our marriages, we must commit to having open lines of communication with one another at all times (yes, in the good and in the bad). We must commit to working towards having effective, productive, and healthy marital communication. Effective communication allows both parties to be heard, allows both parties to agree to disagree, and entails boundaries or lines that both parties have agreed not to cross no matter what. Boundaries are crucial during those times when spouses are engaged in conflict and can easily be led to respond based on their emotions. Productive communication allows both parties to feel as if their voice was heard and their perspective and ideas were communicated calmly. It also allows you to talk to one another, not at one another. Healthy communication permits us to feel respected, loved, and valued.

Communication has been one of the challenges in our marriage. For the most part, our parents did not model for us what productive and healthy communication looked like in a marriage. Our parents taught us as best as they knew how. As a result, we learned better communication skills in our marriage through trial and error. To this day we are still a work in progress. On any given day, we still battle with what was actually intended when we opened up our mouth and what was actually perceived, the non-verbal that was communicated vs. the actual words that were spoken.

Tone has also played a role in our communication. There have been times when communication failed before it even got started based on our tone. There are times when we both have engaged in communication that had undertones of sarcasm, disrespect, lack of consideration, raised/elevated tone, and even a tone of "whatever." When communication is non-existent or has ceased, the survival rate of your marriage is at risk. When there are open lines of communication, your marriage can continue to grow and flourish.

Knowing our communication pattern is extremely important in our marriage. We must be in touch with and admit to the unhealthy examples that were modeled for us so that we can change our own pattern of communication. There was a time when I resided with my grandparents as a young girl. My grandparents had a love-hate type of marital relationship. The communication between the two of them was broken and bitter. There were many times when they communicated with name-calling and the use of profane language. This became a state of normalcy for them based on the unresolved conflict in their marriage. Realizing that my exposure to such marital communication shaped my pattern of communication, allowed me to know my flaws and where I needed to put in the work.

Statistics support that many marriages fail because the two spouses have given up on communicating. They have allowed their past poor communication or miscommunication to infiltrate their present. Communication is, in fact, the lifeline in the marriage. The moment that spouses decide to stop communicating is the moment at which the marriage begins to die. When communication ceases in a marriage, seeking outside help is mandatory in order for the marriage to survive. It is okay (and we urge you) to seek marriage counseling, spiritual counseling or a third trusted, unbiased party to serve as a mediator to assist in restoring and healing the communication in your marriage. Communication in Kingdom marriages is targeted by the enemy who desires to demolish and destroy the family. We must know who our real enemy is and commit to doing everything within our power to save our marriage and be willing to put in the work to do so! I Declare and Decree that your marriage will not die!

PRAYER

God, I lift up every spouse and every marriage that has or is experiencing broken, dead, non-existent, unhealthy communication. I speak healing and wholeness into their mind, their mouths, and into their memories. Their marriages will live and not die. I come against every statistic, every generational curse, every negative word, every naysayer, and every societal norm that has said that marriages will fail, communication will fail, and the marriage will end in divorce. What you have joined together nothing can put asunder! I plead the blood of Jesus over their mouths, their minds, and their marriage covenant. I declare that the cycle of miscommunication has been broken, and healing is taking place right NOW.

God, I ask that you break generational curses and create new and healthy norms of communication in every bloodline and in every marriage, in Jesus' name!!!

Wow Moment Reflection

> *"Love is patient, love is kind. It does not envy, it does not boast, it is not proud."*
>
> (1 Corinthians 13:4 **NIV**)

KEY #10

TAKE THE TIME TO LEARN AND KNOW EACH OTHER'S NEEDS IN THE MARRIAGE

As we know, throughout most of Chapter 13 in 1 Corinthians God is referring to love and what it really means. So it is fitting that we take into consideration that God is giving us a blueprint of how we should love each, especially in our marriages. The first thing we read is, "Love is patient." When we take time to learn and know each other's needs, patience is going to be a true starting place or key factor because we have to understand that it is the other person's needs that we want to learn. At times that can be totally different than what we think or imagine. Patience is a huge selfless act that we all must display in our relationships, period, because we are in that position called "dependence" of someone else to act, say, or think. We depend on our spouse to help us to be clear about what it is they need in the relationship, not what we want to give them.

We often times make decisions based on "our wants for our spouse's needs," but we have to understand that it is "their needs that we should want" in order to make that decision. When we go there, we tackle the second part of the scripture,

"Love is kind." As a married couple, at ALL TIMES we have to realize kindness is how we should relate and act towards one another. Are there times that we get angry with each other? Yes! It is a part of the growth of the relationship. But angry does not mean you have the open door to unkindness. Anger is a feeling or emotion, and kindness is an action or an attitude. There is a quote or mantra my wife and I live by, **"Attitude is Everything"** (Dr. Patricia D. Hatten). So if you look at attitude being everything, then kindness should be significant in your relationship, especially when you are learning about each other's needs.

How can you be mean to your spouse or even not have patience when you are saying, "I want to know what you need in our relationship"? The scripture goes on talking about love does not envy, does not boast and is not proud. What God is saying here is that we should not make the other person feel like we are not happy about their successes or even make them feel unhappy about ours. In marriage, it is about oneness. In learning or knowing what your spouse's needs are, you should always make them feel like you are proud of them as they should be of you. If you are often learning what each other's needs are, being envious should never be an issue because you will not have the time to be resentful of your spouse. The independent qualities within the relationship only make your UNION more exceptional, not your independence. You, again, are one -- or becoming one -- which simply means that you are each other, and your strengths put together make your marriage STRONG.

When we are working towards knowing each other's needs, it is all about what you want from me as your spouse, what you want from life as your life-long partner, and even what you want spiritually as your spiritual tie with God being our helper. So when you look at it that way, what each other's needs are should be an ongoing routine that you constantly consider as your relationship grows. Needs and wants are always changing as we mature. To think that what she or he needed from me at the beginning of our relationship is the same now that we are years down the road together is never going to work. As God says, love patiently. Love with kindness. Do this while taking the time to know each other's needs. You will find it is as essential as taking the time to grow. They go hand-in-hand.

PRAYER

Dear Amazing God, we want to thank you for your many blessings as well as your grace. Lord, you have told us in your word how to love, and we understand that love is, first, patient. As we live out our lives together, we should see clearly how important patience is, because you are the true example of how love has to have patience through how you continue to love us despite our faults and shortcomings. Lord, teach us how to know and love each other like husbands and wives should. Teach us how to be examples for our children and the world. Remind us how important it is to know each other's needs and desires over our own within our marriage. Teach us how to be mindful of our covenant to each other daily. Teach us how to desire each other's heart as we continue to become one. Lord, we thank you for your divine purpose for us to be a married couple. For we understand that marriage is your design for a man and woman alone, and we rebuke every plot, plan, and scheme of the enemy! There is no weapon that is formed against us that shall prosper! We declare and decree this, in the precious name of Jesus the Christ. Amen!

Wow Moment Reflection

> *"My dear brothers and sisters, take note of this: Everyone should be quick to listen, slow to speak and slow to become angry."*

(James 1:19 **NIV**)

KEY #11

LISTEN INSTEAD OF THINKING

As we go through life, especially while we are married, we find that communication is one of the important, if not the most important, parts in our relationships. In our theme scripture for this key, the word of God is undoubtedly making it clear that listening is the first stage. It says that we SHOULD be quick to listen, which means that when you are communicating with your spouse, the first consideration is to listen. Most times we want to respond, or we are preparing our answers in our minds. In doing so, we are not truly listening. Thinking instead of listening can cause our response to be off or pointless, because it may not be anywhere near what the conversation is really about. There are other times when we are so-called communicating with our spouse that we hear words that we attach to attitudes or problems. When we do this, it automatically sends a signal to our minds to take a defensive approach.

Every time someone comes to us with anger or hyper actions, we immediately go there and become angry or hyper as well. Our defense mechanism automatically kicks in, in these instances. However, if we take the time to just listen to what is actually being said to us or how the communication is really going, there will be far fewer arguments in the marriage than necessary. God tells us, "Slow to answer and slow to be angry." Listening allows us to slow down our desires to answer and definitely slow or even remove our anger. Two people that love one another should always speak with compassion and thoughtfulness towards each other even while being upset. Even when we are upset with our spouse, we should still speak to him/her with kindness and listen with understanding. The easy thing to do is to think that because he/she is angry that they are going to say hurtful things. What is really hurtful is the assumption of what isn't really being said or the fact that you truly did not take time to listen to who was talking.

Again, communication is essential and can be the very thing that bonds you together with your spouse. Listening within that communication is what makes the bond tighter because you HEAR intently what your spouse is saying and not think about what or how you will respond. God wants us to listen when He speaks. And, believe it or not, God listens to us when we pray. It is important to LISTEN. You just might hear something you really need to know!

PRAYER

Dear Gracious God, we want to thank you, oh, God, for this opportunity to talk to you directly. We know, oh, God, that you can answer our prayers before we even open our mouths, but you love the communication. So we understand your word tells us to be quick to listen, and we believe that you are listening to us speak when our hearts talk, our spirits talk, and when we say something in our minds. We also believe that when you speak, your words are so crystal clear and from your heart that we cannot do anything but listen. And we thank you for the clarity of your voice. Teach us how we are to be great listeners in our marriages and relationships so that we can hear our spouse's heart and not just their words. Help us to be slow to answer and slow to be angry in order for our relationships to have an effective communicational base. We thank you for the many blessing through our act of listening. In the name of your son Jesus the Christ, Amen!

Wow Moment Reflection

"And the man and his wife were both naked and were not ashamed or embarrassed."

(Genesis 2:25 **AMP**)

KEY #12

DON'T KEEP SECRETS: PRACTICE TRANSPARENCY

In Genesis Chapter 2 we find that Adam and Eve were created in an environment and atmosphere of spiritual and literal nakedness and exposure. In this natural state, they operated in a place of being both unashamed and transparent. They were naked and not ashamed. This is the natural state that God had intended for them. In this state they found themselves lured and deceived into a place of secrecy. As an adjective, <u>secret</u> is defined as "something that is hidden or concealed." Other words or synonyms for <u>secret</u> include "undisclosed, private, or unknown."

The bible first introduces us to the idea of secrets, secrecy, or hidden things in the book of Genesis Chapter 3 where we find the story of Adam and Eve. In this text, we read about how Eve is being persuaded and convinced by the serpent to eat of the forbidden tree. Not only does Eve disobey God's command and eats from the forbidden tree, but she then gives some of the forbidden fruit to her husband who also decides to eat it. Out of their disobedience, the two lose their purity and innocence and become shameful in their nakedness. They attempt to cover themselves by tying fig leaves together as clothing. Also, out of their disobedience, they attempt to **hide** from their creator, God, in **secrecy** and become spiritually separated from God by their sin. Their original state of unashamedly walking in nakedness and in spiritual harmony was forfeited.

Marriage is a covenant with a goal of two becoming one, operating in harmony and transparency. Secrecy is something that should never enter the covenant of marriage. Our marriages should be grounded and rooted in transparency. Secrets are things we are often lured and deceived to partake in. But we individually make a conscious decision to voluntarily and of our own free will participate and engage in such activity. We make a decision to keep a person, a thing, or even a situation hidden from our covenant partner. Secrets in marriage create a wedge between a husband and wife that is often hard to penetrate. Maintaining a secret leads to a domino effect of repetitive acts of secrecy and can even spiral out of control.

Secrets in a marriage will not end well and will result in destruction, distrust, and division in your marriage. The enemy's goal and purpose in life is to create a wedge in your covenant. Examples of secrecy in your marriage include: maintaining secret friends, making secret purchases, having secret friendships or relationships, giving or lending money in secret, having a secret crush, having an unknown bank account, secret illness, etc. These are all destructive to your marriage. God calls husbands and wives to walk in unity, to operate in transparency, and to coexist in nakedness and not be ashamed.

During a tumultuous and dark time in our own marriage, we experienced a period where we were tricked and lured into secrecy and deception by the enemy. It is during the times in our marriage when we are facing challenges, loss, lack, perceived isolation, or even disappointment that we can become vulnerable and targeted by the enemy for spiritual separation from our spouse and even from God. No marriage is exempt from this or any other scheme of the enemy, and it is to our own benefit that we become aware of the enemy's strategies so that we can develop a plan of defense. In our marriage, during our challenging season, the transparency in certain areas of our covenant was truly compromised and we no longer operated in a place of harmony and unity.

Most of the time we operated in silo. Instead of running towards one another, we ran away from one another. Instead of disclosing things, we hid things. Instead of engaging one another, we retreated and operated in silo, and our actions and behaviors promoted dishonesty, secrecy, and hidden things, instead of transparency and nakedness. This was a very unfulfilling and unfruitful time in our marriage. In retrospect, we realize that we allowed the enemy to steal precious moments from us that can never be regained. During this season in our marriage, contrary to God's desire and purpose for marriage, our behaviors fostered a lack of peace and happiness, and our disobedience delayed and held up our blessings. It wasn't until we admitted our faults, disclosed our secrets, prayed and came together before God with a repentant heart that our marriage was able to move towards mending, renewal, and spiritual harmony.

In our marriages, we have to guard ourselves against anything or anyone that promotes or causes us to get out of unity and fellowship with our spouse. Anyone or anything that encourages secrecy, hiding, or withholding information or things in your marriage should be ousted from your covenant. These persons and things should be cut off immediately before they take root. Godly counsel will point you back to God and the God idea of marriage. Godly counsel promotes oneness in marriage. Husbands and wives are charged with cleaving to one another, being honest and transparent with one another, sticking one to another, and pursuing prayer at all times (in season and out of season)!

PRAYER

God, we come seeking you with our whole heart like never before. We need you to show up in our lives and in our marriage today. God, we are asking you to intervene in our covenant and demonstrate your power and your perfect will for us. God, help us to set aside our fleshly and worldly desires and mindset so that we can hear and be obedient to your commands as it relates to our marriage. Cleanse us of every worldly thought and idea that would hinder us from operating in transparency with our spouse. God help us to be willing to walk in forgiveness and to wipe the slate clean and begin anew in and with you. Empower us with your word and with your anointing, that we would be able to withstand all the wiles of the enemy. Your word reminds us that nothing is too hard for you, and nothing is impossible to them that believe. We believe you! We claim the victory and vow to walk in transparency with our spouse. In Jesus' name, Amen!

Wow Moment Reflection

"Let all that you do be done in love."

(1 Corinthians 16:14 **ESV**)

KEY #13

STAY ROMANTIC

In 1 Corinthians 16:14 God keeps it simple and clear by telling us that everything we do we are to make sure it is done in love. Even though this key is titled "Stay Romantic," when you look at the definition of romantic, it relates to LOVE. The definition states, "conducive to or characterized by the expression of love." Even the synonym of romantic is "loving and passionate." So of course, it is fitting to use one of the main books in the bible that talks about LOVE in discussing this key. In the courting stages of marriage, we intentionally do so much and beyond in order to romance our soon-to-be husband or wife. For example, we cook candlelight dinners for each other, we play or sing "our favorite" song for each other, we buy flowers for each other, and we even take overnight trips with each other. When we reach the stage of married, many of us sometimes forget that those are the things that made the courting moments toward marriage so amazing and made us feel as if we could not wait to be married.

So staying romantic is truly necessary for our marriage because it allows the flame to remain lit as well as the love to grow. Even when we change the word "Romantic" to "Romance," the definition does not change much. As we know, it states, "a feeling of excitement and mystery associated with love." Staying romantic with each other -- take notice that I said, **"WITH EACH OTHER,"** which is not a one-sided concept -- should definitely have excitement involved. Excitement is sometimes doing the WOW-Factor. Staying romantic goes back to understanding your spouse's love language (Key #6). It is what makes them know and feel you love them. But adding romance can cause the language to be crystal clear. Being romantic does not mean bedroom activity, but it definitely can promote it.

We must also understand that romantic and/or romance does not necessarily mean spending money. Romance does not mean expenses. To be romantic does not mean you have to take that cruise or eat at a five-star restaurant. Simply stated, romance is your actions and thoughtfulness that comes directly from your heart. We often hear, "It is not the gift that counts, but it is the thought behind it." Well, when you are staying romantic in your marriage, every part should be a thoughtful act from your heart and spirit. Your wallet or bank account has not attached itself to your spouse. So why should it be the thing you go to, to help you display your affection?

Your spouse's five-star restaurant meal just may be you home cooking their favorite foods. Their best vacation trip could very well be a quiet house with an ocean wave soundtrack playing in the background while you are cuddling by the fireplace. Okay, you may be saying, "Well, we have children in the house, so how can we have candlelight dinners or be romantic without leaving the house with them around?" Well, your children can actually play a part in the candlelight dinners by playing the roles of the waiter and/or waitress. They can help prepare the table. They can help with serving the food, and they can even help with making sure the music does not stop playing in the background. In fact, children enjoy seeing mom and dad being romantic, just not the bedroom activity. Involving the children can play a big part in the romance because it allows them to understand that what is going on is all about love and how much you love each other, especially if they, too, can feel it.

Remember, romance is not sexual, because it is the reaction of the heart that causes you to be creative outside of the bedroom, not the action of the body that is created inside the bedroom. Consider it as it should be presented, which is your response to what the word of God says, "Let all that you do be done in love." Romance should be present, and it should stay present in your marriage!

PRAYER

Dear Father God, we thank you for this understanding that everything we do must be done in love. Allow the romance between my spouse and me to remain and be creative to allow our love to grow daily. We seek out wisdom enough to know how to be romantic, how to be out-of-the-box thinkers and be overwhelmingly spontaneous with each other. Let us not forget how we first fell in love, so that we can remain in love forever. In Jesus' name, Amen!

Wow Moment Reflection

> *"Be good friends who love deeply; practice playing second fiddle."*
>
> (Romans 12:10b **MSG**)

KEY #14

DATE YOUR SPOUSE REGULARLY

According to the *Oxford Living Dictionary*, date is defined as "a social or romantic appointment or engagement." It is imperative for married couples to pursue romance through dating after the wedding vows have been said, the honeymoon has ended, the newness has worn off, and the kids are born. Before marriage, couples tend to spend a lot of time dating one another, including spending time intentionally doing things that are fun, sociable, adventurous, interesting, impressionable, and enjoyable. Both the man and woman make it a priority to dress to impress, to smell good, and to go to the beauty salon/barbershop so that they can present their best self to their significant other. Couples look forward to their routine date night, and they aim to please and to spend as much time as they can with one another. It is during the dating phase that couples get the opportunity to bond and grow closer, and to learn and experience the characteristics of the other person when their guard is down.

What happened to dating after the wedding? What happened to dressing to impress after the wedding? Many couples fail to prioritize dating in the marriage, and they tend to slack off of the dating phase, resulting in the relationship becoming routine, dull, stale, and mundane. Romance tends to take a back seat to work, bills, chores, the kids, and other obligations. After the wedding, there doesn't seem to be enough time to fit dating into the schedule. Dating tends to take a back seat after marriage, and it isn't viewed as vital as it was before the formal commitment of "till death do us part." Why is that? Common responses are: my spouse knows that I love him/her, I am pursuing my career, complacency, and taking the other for granted. These and similar responses for not dating after marriage, unfortunately, will result in a broken and dying marriage. Failing to date after marriage could harm your marriage, cause your love to fade and your relationship to drift apart.

There are various reasons to continue dating after marriage. Successful and prosperous marriages don't just happen. Dating your spouse regularly helps to fuel the flame in the marriage, draws you closer to one another, and reminds you why the two of you came together. Dating your spouse strengthens your union. Dating allows you to build new shared memories together and the opportunity to discover new interests. Dating also helps to draw you and your spouse closer together to continue the goal of oneness in your marriage. It is only by investing and spending time together that the marriage, blossoms, grows, and evolves.

Romans 12:10 (MSG) instructs us to be good friends and to practice being less important and putting the other person first. God desires for spouses to have a solid friendship. Your friendship with your spouse is most important and is nurtured and maintained when time is invested in your spouse. When we put our spouse in a position greater than ourselves, it humbles us and causes us to want to fulfill their needs, their wants, and desires ahead of our own. Dating your spouse lets him/her know that they are a priority in your life and that they are loved. Your friendship with your spouse is nurtured as the two of you commit to dating and spending quality time together. Take the time to greet one another with love, affection, and excitement! Surprise one another with gifts and small tokens of appreciation. Happy dating!

PRAYER

God, we commit to dating in our marriage! Help us to prioritize and make time to date our spouse! Help us to have fun and to enjoy one another's company. Holy Spirit, we invite you into this renewed commitment to dating in our marriage. We declare that we will be intentional about laughing, loving, and celebrating one another. Marriage is your idea, and we want to please you in all that we do. Empower us, renew us, and strengthen us, in Jesus' name!

Wow Moment Reflection

> *"That is why a man leaves his father and mother and is united to his wife, and they become one flesh."*

(Genesis 2:24 **NIV**)

KEY #15

MAINTAIN THE MINDSET THAT SPENDING TIME TOGETHER IS IMPORTANT

God's word is clear when it comes to what happens when a man and a woman unite. United is defined as "joined together politically, for a common purpose, or by common feelings." Some of the synonyms that we can use include: joined, merged, and the one I like is like-minded. The scripture goes on to say, we should become "one flesh." So according to this phrase, if you are truly trying to become one with your spouse, your mindset should be making things priority and spending time together, which plays a vital role in the marriage. Although the scripture does not reference spending time with your spouse, it does indicate that a man leaves his father and mother. Let's understand what God is saying so that we are not confused. God is not saying, leave your parents and not care for them or not have a relationship with them. He is saying there is a person that is now in position that requires top priority in your life.

It then says, "And they become one flesh." This means that as your relationship with your spouse grows, you should see her or him as you see yourself. She/he should be just as important to you as you are to yourself. When she/he is hurting, you should be reacting in that hurt. When you are happy, you should be assuring that she/he is feeling happy. The word <u>mindset</u> is defined as "the established set of attitudes held by someone." When I say, "maintain the mindset," I am boldly saying that you should establish an attitude that you are going to make it important and a priority to spend time with your spouse.

We are always prioritizing things in our careers, our education, and even with our children. Therefore, it is highly important to prioritize your time for your spouse. Before marriage, you did those things to show her/him how much you wanted to be in their presence and did whatever was necessary to make it happen. After marriage, you must do the same! I am not talking about continuing to date her/him, which is also important. I am talking about intentionally setting quality time, not just quantity time. Making her/him a requirement, not a routine, and grow in the relationship, not groaning in the relationship.

PRAYER

Heavenly Father, we come first giving praise and honor to your holy name. We thank you, oh, Lord, for allowing us to have this opportunity to come with direct access to you, and we ask that your presence be felt in this moment. Gracious God, we ask that you keep us mindful of how our relationship with each other is important and that spending time together to grow, learn, and understand each other is just as important. Our time together allows us to grow into that oneness that you seek and desire for our relationship, and we ask that as our minds focus on that concept, that our hearts also align with that same thought. Thank you for granting us the time, because we know that we are not promised tomorrow nor the next second in this thing we call life. So keep us under your will and your way for our marriage and our lives. In Jesus' name we pray. Amen!

Wow Moment Reflection

> *"Above all, love each other deeply, because love covers over a multitude of sins."*
>
> (1 Peter 4:8 **NIV**)

KEY #16

EXPRESS LOVE AND AFFECTION TOWARDS YOUR SPOUSE DAILY

John 3:16 (KJV) tells us, "For God so loved the world, that he gave his only begotten Son, that whosoever believeth in him should not perish, but have everlasting life." God demonstrated for us and provided the ultimate example of love for God's people by giving His only son to die on the cross for the sins we had not yet committed to give us the ability to possess eternal life. Now that's **LOVE**. The word "love" in Hebrew is *Ahava*, and it means, "I give" and "love." To love means to give. We should love our spouses such that we would be willing to sacrifice our life on their behalf. You cannot profess to love someone and not give of yourself unconditionally. You cannot profess to love someone and not want to give them that which brings them joy. Love is giving of oneself sacrificially. Love is selfless, not selfish. To love in marriage means to be concerned about the welfare and interest of our spouse and not just our own. Sacrificial love puts the needs of your spouse above and before your own. Sacrificial love gives until it hurts, gives until the other is fulfilled, and gives until there is nothing else to give.

Love also covers. The Greek word for cover means "to hide; to cover with a veil." *Dictionary.com* defines hide as "to conceal from knowledge or exposure; to keep secret." In essence, love covers and hides. Love covers and hides the faults, the shortcomings, the mishaps, the mistakes, and even the sins of your spouse. Just as love covers, love forgives. Love forgives such that the sins committed by your spouse are hidden and do not have a stronghold in your marriage; thereby causing a lack of unity, chaos, and turmoil. This does not mean that you deny the fact that your spouse sinned or committed an offense against you. It means that you covered your spouse's sin with forgiveness, rendering the sin or offense powerless in your marriage.

Not every marriage is rooted in love. Our marriages go through seasons where there may be times when a given marriage lacks love (forgiveness, a covering). A lack of love can manifest itself in many ways in a marriage, including laziness, disrespect, disregard, lack of affection, irritability, snappiness, silent treatment, no sex, etc. This is not biblical and is not God's will for our marriage. In fact, John 15:12 (NIV) says, "My command is this: Love each other as I have loved you." God loved us enough that God sent his son to die on the cross to cover our sins.

PRAYER

Lord, teach us how to love our spouse unconditionally. Teach every husband and every wife how to honor their spouse's love language and to love their spouse the way they not only want to be loved but deserve and need to be loved. Instruct us, Lord, in spite of our past, our previous unhealthy demonstrations of love by society and our own family, and even our negative thoughts that often try to overtake us. Teach us how to love our spouse to the point that our love covers their sins, their failures, their disappointments, their hurts, and their offenses. Lord, I ask you to personally help ME to love my spouse deeply and to cover my spouse in prayer daily.

Wow Moment Reflection

"He who finds a wife finds what is good and receives favor from the Lord."

(Proverbs 18:22 **NIV**)

KEY #17

COMPLIMENT EACH OTHER OFTEN

In Proverbs 18 verse 22, the Lord is letting us know that whenever a man receives a wife, it is favor from the Lord. That statement alone is strong enough to give us clarity regarding how the Lord sees a wife to a man and how much the Lord sees the man to a wife. The wife is God's favor to the man. And if she is favor to him from the Lord, then the man is seen as someone whom God loves. Just sit back and take that in for a moment. God is giving a man FAVOR when God gives him a wife. Then consider this thought: if God is calling her His favor, then she is someone precious and valuable.

The definition of favor as a noun means "an act of kindness beyond what is due or usual." The verb tense is defined as "feel or show approval or preference for." When we look at both descriptions of the word, we see that God is taking this serious enough to use it in both forms. He is showing an act of kindness beyond what is due to men first (the gift/wife). Remember, Romans 3:23, "For all have sinned and fall short of the glory of God" (NIV). God is giving the man a gift/wife even though, in the world's eye, he is not worthy of this gift. Then God shows His approval of the man by his actions of giving the favor, which God is saying in Psalm 149:4, "For the Lord taketh pleasure in his people: he will beautify the meek with salvation" (KJV). Again, God is telling the world, I know what you see, but I am pleased with him enough to give him favor.

I remember growing up as a little boy, and whenever my parents would give me something or would show me favor over someone else, it would make my day, my week, or even my year, depending on what it was. The gift or the favor would also be cherished in every way possible. So when God gives you favor, men, it is simply Him truly thinking of you for this particular gift or moment in your life. In this case, it is in the form of a wife. She is handpicked by God! God created and made someone just for you and you for her! As the saying goes, what God has for me is for ME! We often pray and ask God for His favor and blessings. But in this particular scripture God is telling us that even if we have not prayed for a wife or a husband, let alone to be married, that when He allows this to happen to us, we should NEVER categorize it as a ball-and-chain, a trap from living a free life, or even a hindrance. What favor from God can ever be considered a bad thing?

What kind of God would create you, call you blessed, send His son to die for you, and then give you a gift in the form of a spouse and it be such a bad thing? A man and woman are wonderfully made. They are a child of God. The wife is, as it says, a favor from the Lord, and we should treat her as such. And he is the man God set aside and set apart just for you. She should hear how beautiful she is OFTEN. He should hear how handsome he is OFTEN. She should hear how much she lights up the room, how much you see her as your queen. The man should hear how much he is needed in your life and how much you see him as your king. If we are not complimenting our spouse after our great God has put us together, the enemy will set up that opposition in this area. He will have that someone to take the **initiative** (*the power or opportunity to act or take charge before others do*) to say something to your spouse that he or she desires from you. We should see and say something special to each other every day!

Remember the love languages (Key #6). It is an expectation in marriages! It sends the message, "I notice you!" It provides the mindset to your spouse that you are paying attention to them. How awesome it is to have the man that God is pleased with to tell you how much he desires you. How wonderful is it to have that woman that God calls blessed to tell you how she has butterflies when you walk in the room. Fall in love again through compliments from the heart for each other.

PRAYER

Dear Amazing God, we thank you for the gift of life and the gift of love. We ask, oh, God, that you give us the ability to tell each other how much we see each other through the same eyes you see us. You see us as blessed, and beautifully and wonderfully made. Let us be mindful of our spouses every day that we have each other. Let the love that we have for each other saturate our marriage overwhelmingly so that there is no room for the enemy to separate. We say what you say, "There is no weapon that is formed against us that shall prosper!" Thank you, oh, Lord, for keeping us together and keeping us strong. In Jesus' name, Amen!

Wow Moment Reflection

> *"'In your anger do not sin': Do not let the sun go down while you are still angry."*
>
> (Ephesians 4:26 **NIV**)

KEY #18

NEVER GO TO BED ANGRY

In this text, Paul is teaching us that getting angry is not wrong, and anger in and of itself is not sinful. In John Chapter 2, we see that Jesus even became angry and demonstrated His anger when He turned over the tables of the tax collectors. Let's start right there with this mindset. God is making it clear to us that anger is not a sin, but lingering and prolonged anger can lead to sin. If we want to please God, we have to mentally and spiritually understand what sin will do to our relationship with God. Although the Word tells us to repent of our sins, and God is just to forgive us, we still have to maintain a focus of staying away from what we know is a sin.

Anger that lingers in our marriage plays a significant role that God is not pleased with. First, ask yourself, aren't we all considered to be God's children? Then say, isn't Jesus God's son as well? So being angry with one of God's children sounds like you can even be angry with Jesus the Son of God. Now ask the real question, "Can I really be angry with Jesus or any of God's children?" If your answer is no, then letting the sun go down while you are angry should not even be a thought or consideration. Do we have disagreements or get frustrated with our spouses? Yes! Even with this being true for everyone, we still have to figure out how we are not pleasing God with harboring anger against His child. God's word, again, is our saving grace, because He knows we will get angry with each other. Instead of telling us how hurt the anger makes Him feel, He simply says, don't allow too much time to go by without resolving your anger.

Again, it is the lingering of the anger which God sees as sin and not the act of being angry. Now that we have identified God's point of view on the matter, let's talk about what it does to us as individuals. When we get angry with our spouses, we should ask ourselves, What type of message are we really delivering? Are we angry with them for who and what they are to us, or are we angry with what was said or done, which are two separate concepts? If we are angry at who or what they are to us, no matter what they say or do will ever be good enough. We see them and treat them as an enemy and not as someone we love and cherish. If this is true, then lingering anger is inevitable even longer than the sun going down. If you are angry at what was said or done, then we are seeing the true enemy at his best in our relationship.

The devil loves a separated household and a torn marriage because marriage is a God-ordained covenant for man and woman. Understanding that arguments and disagreements are a plot, plan, and trick of the enemy is why we need to find and pursue peace in the home and peace in our marriages.

Lingering anger allows the door to remain open for the real ENEMY not only to enter but to reside.

PRAYER

Dear All forgiving Lord and Savior, we come before you asking for your forgiveness for ALL sin that we have committed by word, thought, and deed. We ask that those sins never stand in the way of you blessing us in our marriages and in our lives. We seek out deliverance from anger, rage, and bitterness so that we might be humbled enough to be kind to each other at all times and in all situations. Oh, God, teach us to how to act, think, and talk, in the name of Jesus. Teach us how to react and communicate with each other in the name of Jesus. Shower us with your love, your grace, and your mercy, that we may stay in your will. Give us a kind heart for each other. We thank you for your joy and your peace. You said in your word, "For God is not a God of disorder but of peace," and we thank you for your PEACE, in Jesus' name. Amen!

Wow Moment Reflection

> *"And then God answered: 'Write this. Write what you see. Write it out in big block letters so that it can be read on the run. This vision-message is a witness pointing to what's coming. It aches for the coming—it can hardly wait! And it doesn't lie. If it seems slow in coming, wait. It's on its way. It will come right on time.'"*
>
> (Habakkuk 2:2-3 **MSG**)

KEY #19

HAVE A VISION STATEMENT FOR YOUR MARRIAGE

Habakkuk 2:2-3 is a very familiar scripture that is often used when talking about creating a vision board or creating and writing goals for your life. This scripture gives specific instructions to the prophet to write it down. In the bible, whenever the prophets were commanded to *write* anything, it represented the significance of it, and that the fulfilling of it was at some distance or future time appointed by God. Based on this scripture, when developing our goals, we, too, are strongly encouraged to write out exactly what we desire to see and to accomplish. When creating a vision board, we are instructed to use pictures, words, and images that reflect exactly what it is we desire to achieve in a particular year or in a set period of time.

Goals are a map to guide you to your God-given purpose and destiny. Research supports that people who write down their goals are more likely to accomplish them. In fact, research reflects that those who write down their dreams and goals regularly tend to achieve their goals at a significantly higher rate than those who don't. On the other hand, a vision board is a tool used to assist in clarifying specific goals and displays images that represent those things one wants to be or to accomplish in their life. A vision is a visual picture that serves to remind you of that which you have set out to accomplish. In essence, your vision board allows you to see it before you actually achieve it.

In considering what has already been outlined above, we have noticed that, in general, society highly recommends and strongly encourages us to set, write goals, and to create a vision board for our life, but the same momentum and energy to do so in and for our marriage is lacking. Why do we put so much effort and energy into our individual life and not put that same effort and energy into our marriage? Statistics reflect that less than 3% of married couples actually set goals for their marriage. I would imagine that there are less married couples than that who take on the challenge to write a vision statement for their marriage. At the 50% failure rate of marriages, and Kingdom marriages specifically, for this reason, we have identified this as one of the most essential keys in this book. Creating a vision statement and setting goals for your marriage is not just recommended, BUT we believe that it is necessary in order to create the marriage that you desire to experience with God's help.

We wrote our very first vision statement for our marriage over ten years ago after being married for over 16 years. It was only after we began conducting pre-marital education sessions that we embraced the idea and saw the value in writing the vision and making it plain in our marriage. Doing so changed us individually and collectively, and the direction and evolution of our marriage are credited to this process. There's something about formally establishing a written plan for your marriage, rooted and established in your faith that God honors. In essence, a marriage vision statement focuses on creating that which does not yet exist, with the help, the leading, and the empowerment of God. We wrote what we wanted to see and experience in our marriage, and today we see the manifestation of that vision.

We want to invite you to take the time to write your marriage goals and your marriage vision statement. It doesn't matter if you have been married for 6 months or 60 years. Start this process right where you are NOW. We face so many challenges in our marriages that we have to be intentional about building the marriage we want to see and the legacy that we want to leave. You can begin this process by writing at least 10 goals you want to achieve in your marriage over the next three to five years. Your goals can be used to develop and formulate your marriage vision statement. Your vision statement should be both specific and positive. Choose at least one foundational scripture that supports your vision statement and include it. Remember, vision is that which is invisible and making it visible. Once finalized, we encourage you to review your vision statement and your goals at least every quarter to tweak or to start anew as applicable.

As you embark upon this process, we wanted to share our very first vision statement with you to encourage you as you take on the challenge to write out your vision in BIG-block-letters.

Dunston Marriage Vision Statement

"We will have a God-centered marriage that is sustained by Respect, Love, Integrity, and Joy. Our Marriage will exemplify Unity and Oneness, setting a Godly example for others to follow. We are committed to Encouraging, Supporting and Praying for and with one another daily. We are dedicated to Nurturing and Strengthening our marriage by spending quality time with one another where true intimacy dwells. With the help of the Holy Spirit, we will honor the covenant we made before God."

Ecclesiastes 4:12 (KJV)

"And if one prevail against him, two shall withstand him; and a threefold cord is not quickly broken."

Psalm 106:45(a) (MSG)

"He remembered his covenant with them, and, immense with love, took them by the hand."

PRAYER

Lord, as we embark upon writing down what we want to experience and see in our marriage, we ask for your direction, your power, and your anointing throughout this process. Speak to us so that we might hear your vision and not our vision. Remind us why you put us together in the first place. Your word says to write the vision and make it plain. As we are obedient to your word, Lord, allow the vision to come to pass at your appointed time that you will be glorified. Allow others to see you in us and in our covenant. In Jesus' name, Amen!

Wow Moment Reflection

"The Lord is far from the wicked, but he hears the prayer of the righteous."

(Proverbs 15:29 **NIV**)

KEY #20

PRIORITIZE PRAYER IN YOUR MARRIAGE

(HIS VIEW)

It is imperative that we understand how important prayer is in our own individual lives and even more important in our marriage. Prayer is communication with God and is a significant part of our relationship with God. As a young married man, I did not prioritize prayer in my marriage, but I knew that my wife did. It was not that I did not think about praying with her, it just was not something I made an effort to do or prioritized in my marriage. Yes, we attended church together regularly, and yes, we prayed for each other, especially if there was something that the other needed from God. However, it just was not high on my list to do. As my spiritual walk and my relationship with God grew, and my marriage got stronger, prayer became a significant part of my daily routine with my wife.

We started our "TRUE" prayer life together as a married couple by praying together in the mornings on our way to work. We alternate days with regard to who actually leads the prayer. Whenever one of us is struggling to pray, the other just steps right in and leads the prayer. I found that our commitment to prayer as a married couple actually drew me closer to my wife on a spiritual level. Prior to this point, I doubted that I was personally even capable of being a spiritual man or even growing and developing into a more spiritual individual. I am a testament that prayer changes things.

As the scripture tells us in Proverbs 15:29, "The Lord is far from the wicked, but he hears the prayer of the righteous." I understand this scripture to mean that God listens when we pray, and when we pray with faith and believe in Him, He is faithful enough to hear and answer us. So praying for and with my wife is something I enjoy simply because it reminds me that God will not only hear but will respond to my prayer request for my wife. God will surround her with the hedge of protection that I ask for; He will anoint her afresh as requested, and He will open doors for her that no man/woman can close. God's word says in Matthew 7:7-8 "Ask, and it shall be given you; seek, and ye shall find; knock, and it shall be opened unto you: For every one that asketh receiveth; and he that seeketh findeth; and to him that knocketh it shall be opened."

Prayer has definitely gotten us through some difficult times personally, financially, and spiritually. Prioritizing prayer in my marriage saved my marriage! As we prioritize our prayer life with one another, it not only draws us closer together as a married couple, but it draws us closer to God. You have heard how communication is a huge component in a marriage, so it should be quite clear that communication in your marriage with God is even greater and more important. Again, prayer changes and rearranges things and allows heaven and earth to come together. Prioritize prayer in your marriage. I say, "Why Not?" It truly makes a difference!

PRAYER

Dear Gracious God, I come to you on behalf of my spouse, asking, oh, God, that you protect him/her and keep them in perfect peace. You said in your word, oh, God, "My grace is sufficient," so, God, I ask that you shower him/her with your grace and your mercy daily. I ask that you order his/her footsteps and provide him/her with the pathway to your purpose and his/her destiny for his/her life. I say what you say, that there is no weapon that is formed against him/her that shall prosper. Touch his/her body from the top of his/her head to the sole of his/her feet and every organ, blood vessel, and bone in his/her body with a fresh anointing. Oh, God, as he/she submits to your will and your way, I ask that you grant the desires of his/her heart and allow him/her, Heavenly Father, to hear from you. Continue to speak to him/her and through him/her as he/she goes out in the world to preach, teach, and speak to your people what sayeth the Lord.

Comfort him/her, oh, God, as he/she continues to live out your will for their life. Oh, Lord, your word also tells us that where we are weak, your strength is made perfect. So we thank you for your strength and your love for him/her that stands for him/her and with him/her daily. I ask, oh, God, that you bless me to be a blessing to him/her and that you make me the husband/wife that you desire for me to be. I believe in your word in Jeremiah 29:11 that says, "For I know the plans I have for you," declares the Lord, "plans to prosper you and not to harm you, plans to give you hope and a future"… So, Lord, I thank you for your plan that has our name on it. I ask that we be the married couple that you have created us to be, the man and woman that you created us to be, the parents that you created us to be, and most of all, the children of the highest God that you created us to be.

Bind us together in love, and we ask that everything that is not of you be removed from our minds, bodies, and souls. Then pour into us everything that is of you. Fill us up and allow our cups to overflow. Thank you, God, for my husband/wife, and thank you for the many blessings you have given us over the years and will continue to bless us with as we honor you and are obedient to your commands. In Jesus' name, Amen!

Wow Moment Reflection

> *"This is the [remarkable degree of] confidence which we [as believers are entitled to] have before Him: that if we ask anything according to His will, [that is, consistent with His plan and purpose] He hears us."*
>
> (1 John 5:14 **AMP**)

KEY #20

PRIORITIZE PRAYER IN YOUR MARRIAGE

(HER VIEW)

Marriage is not only the first institution created by God as described in the book of Genesis, but it is the most sacred institution on earth that is the foundation for every other institution. As you can imagine, for this reason, the institution of marriage is always under attack. If the enemy can destroy marriages, the enemy can destroy the world and our society. The covenant of marriage is a union that is hated and despised by the enemy and the forces of evil. The enemy despises the potential that exists in marriages because this is a covenant that comes from God. The enemy desires to disrupt, to dismantle, and to destroy this covenant by any means necessary! The enemy knows that where division and confusion exist in a marriage, God's perfect plan, purpose, intentions, and will cannot manifest. The enemy really wants us to abort our covenant assignment through our own actions which would ultimately lead to divorce.

The bible is very clear in telling us that we will experience warfare, but our best defense is to remember that what we fight against is not flesh and blood, but we contend against principalities, against powers, against the rulers of the darkness of this world, and against spiritual wickedness in high places. We must recognize the enemy for who the enemy is and fight the enemy in the spirit and not in the flesh. Your spouse is not your enemy! When we know who the enemy is and the tactics therein, we can exercise our spiritual authority through prayer to defend our covenant with the word of God.

Prayer is our offense and our defense. Prayer is our weapon! Reminding God of God's word in our prayers is a prayer strategy that will work in our favor. God will always honor God's word. Our prayers and petitions for our marriage give God permission to intervene in our affairs, our covenant. Because we know that the enemy is after our covenant, we must commit to praying with and for our husbands regularly, preferably daily. We can tear down the enemy's weapons if we pray. We can dismantle and render the enemy's plots, plans, and schemes powerless against our covenant if we pray. Our prayers do not make us exempt from being under attack by the enemy, but our prayers allow us to partner with God and God to partner with us in fighting the war so that we can win the battle against our marriage.

It is imperative that we pray with and for our spouses. Throughout the day, the enemy throws darts and bait at our husbands to trip them up, to tempt them, to discourage them, to distract them, and to lure them. In our prayers, we must cover our husbands mentally, emotionally, psychologically, socially, spiritually, economically, and physically. We must declare and decree God's word over our spouse so that he can become all that God created him to be. The bible tells us that our words have power, so we must use our authority and speak God's word. God has given us authority over all the power of the enemy. Prayer is required, not optional!

Prayer has made a difference in our marriage. As a result of prayer, we have seen the hand of God work in our favor in our covenant during those times when the enemy crept in and caused confusion, chaos, and division. On several occasions, we have found ourselves fighting to stay in our marriage when we wanted to throw in the towel. During these challenging times, we had to be intentional about not being married to our feelings and honor the word of God to pray. Prayer brings connection and unity in our covenant and opposes the enemy's plan of division.

Even when we are angry with one another, we don't allow the enemy to stop us from coming together to pray. The enemy wants us to remain at odds with one another, to be a house divided, and to view our spouse as the enemy. In our marriage, we come into agreement with God and with one another to pray, because the word of God tells us that the prayers of a righteous man/woman are powerful and effective. God also says that if we ask anything according to

His will, God hears us. Surrender your marriage to God in prayer and watch God honor your prayers.

PRAYER

God, we thank you for being a God of your word. We thank you for being a God that hears and answers our prayers when we pray according to your will. We pray for husbands and wives that they would surrender their covenant to you and commit to praying together and for one another daily. We come against every distraction and disruption that is meant to stop and hinder their commitment to prayer. We declare and decree that husbands and wives will fight the real enemy that is trying to destroy their covenant in the war room of prayer, in Jesus' name, Amen!

Wow Moment Reflection

PRAYER FOR MARRIAGES

God, we come interceding on behalf of marriages today. God, marriage is your idea, and in your word, you said that it is not good for man to be alone. You said, God that a man shall leave his mother and father and be joined to his wife, and the two shall become one flesh. God, you said that what you have joined together, let no man put asunder. Now, God, it is with faith and this understanding that we come praying and standing on your word on behalf of marriages today.

God, we are praying for marriages all over the world and even abroad. We pray for marriages in the making, seasoned marriages, new marriages, hurting marriages, broken marriages, failed marriages, marriages on the brink of a break-up, marriages that are on the crossroads, strained marriages, betrayed marriages, unstable marriages, and even cursed marriages, in Jesus' name! Lord, we come against every demon, every principality, and every form of spiritual wickedness that is assigned to kill and destroy the marriage covenant, in Jesus' name! God, we know that according to your word, we can ask anything in your name.

God, your word says that whatever we bind on earth shall be bound in heaven, and whatever we loose on earth shall be loosed in heaven! God, we bind up the spirit of divorce, in the name of Jesus. God, we bind up adultery and infidelity, in Jesus' name. God, we bind up the home wrecker and all forms of temptation, God, we bind up sexual immorality, lying, deception, financial troubles, pornography, perversion, lust, betrayal, disease, and unforgiveness, in Jesus' name! God, we come against domestic violence of any kind, in Jesus' name! We call the covenant of marriage back into its proper place in the Kingdom of God!

God, we ask that you would release a fresh anointing upon each and every marriage today. God, heal marriages all across the land, in Jesus' name! God, cause husbands and wives to fall back in love with one another, forgive one another, respect, and submit one to another. We ask these things in Jesus' name, Amen!

Wow Moment Reflection

ABOUT THE AUTHORS

Carlton R. Dunston, Jr. is an educator, motivational speaker and a man seeking to empower men to be real with themselves and God. Carlton is affectionately known as "Mr. D" and can be found speaking life into our youth to become what God has called and created them to be through academics and mentoring. Carlton has a unique gift to connect with today's youth in and outside of the classroom. He has a passion for helping our young people "BY ANY MEANS NECESSARY." He is gifted with a spiritual connection to other men and believes that men must take their rightful place as a spiritual leader. He speaks to men with a humble spirit, encouraging them to be proud Kingdom Men as they mature in their walk with God.

Carlton has been a member of Turner Chapel AME Church, Marietta, GA, for more than 17 years and made a bold decision to accept his call to ministry in August 2018. He is currently on the journey of preparation for ordination. He is married to an amazing woman of God, a father to the best two children on earth, and is a daily cheerleader for his family as they strive to fulfill their destiny and God-ordained dreams. He is a native of Philadelphia, PA, and is an alumnus of Peirce College. He is also an alumnus of Kennesaw State University where he received his Bachelor's Degree in Early Childhood Education.

Carlton is the Co-founder of "Divine Destiny and Purpose Ministries," a ministry that was birthed by God through him and his wife, Rev. Theresa Waters-Dunston. This ministry is designed to empower people to become unstuck, unparalyzed, unchained, unlocked, and unleashed by their past to fulfill their life's purpose.

Carlton lives by the word of God found in **Jeremiah 29:11**, "For I know the plans I have for you," declares the LORD, "plans to prosper you and not to harm you, plans to give you hope and a future." He believes that God definitely has a plan for him, and he purposely seeks God out in order to stay within that plan.

Carlton strives to show the world that men are not ashamed to praise God in all situations and in all circumstances. He believes that being a warrior for the Lord is a part of being a man and why God created man!

Reverend Theresa Waters-Dunston is an ordained Elder in the African Methodist Episcopal Church. She is an Associate Minister at Turner Chapel AME Church in Marietta, GA, where she has been a member for more than 17 years and has faithfully served in various leadership roles. Reverend Dunston is married to Carlton Dunston, Jr., and they have two young adult children.

Reverend Dunston is a native of Philadelphia, PA, and graduated Cum Laude from Temple University with a B S. Degree in Criminal Justice. In May 2012, she graduated

Cum Laude from the Interdenominational Theological Center (ITC) with a Master's in Divinity and was nominated for **Who's Who Among Students in American Universities & Colleges**.

In 2013, Reverend Dunston and her husband Brother Carlton birthed "***Divine Destiny & Purpose Ministries***," a global ministry designed to empower people to become unstuck, unparalyzed, unchained, unlocked, and unleashed from the pain of their past, in order to fulfill their life's purpose.

Reverend Dunston is a well-sought-after preacher, mentor, conference host, conference/keynote speaker, and workshop/retreat speaker, among other roles. Reverend Dunston's ministry extends beyond the four walls of her local church. She has ministered to inmates; prepares couples for marriage in her "tell it like it is" premarital education sessions; serves on the Board of Wilfred Stocker Ministries, a ministry designed to meet the needs of people; and has volunteered at the Boys and Girls Club, fulfilling her call to lead people to their God-given destiny.

Reverend Dunston and her husband have an anointed prayer CD, "7 Prayers to Heal Your Soul," host a "Live Your Dreams Motivation Moment" on Facebook, a "First Sundays Monthly Prayer Call," and an annual "Live Your Dreams National Virtual Conference." She is a faithful member of the intercessory prayer team of Love Thy Sistahs global women's ministry. Reverend Dunston is a true worshipper and spirit-filled prayer warrior and intercessor and can be found offering comfort, encouragement, and strength through prayer calls and prayer vigils.

Reverend Dunston's life is a true testament to the resurrecting power of God, and she boldly professes how God turned her *mess* into a *miracle* & her *trials* into a *testimony*! Reverend Dunston truly believes in her call and gives God all the Glory.

CONNECT WITH US

https://www.facebook.com/ddpministries1/

www.twitter.com/ddpministries

www.instagram.com/ddp.ministries

ddp.ministries@yahoo.com

http://www.divinedestinyandpurposeministries.com/

www.ingramcontent.com/pod-product-compliance
Lightning Source LLC
Chambersburg PA
CBHW052056070526
44584CB00017B/2198